W

8/16

L.I.F.E.

Learning Information
For Everyday

Woodstock Public Library
7735 Main Street
Woodstock, GA 30188

L.I.F.E.

Learning Information
For Everyday

Challenge Your Teen's Basic Knowledge

Beth Carey

Beth Carey

L.I.F.E. Learning Information For Everyday

ISBN 978-0-9967548-0-4 (paperback)
ISBN 978-0-9967548-1-1 (eBook)

Library of Congress Control Number: 2015920143

Published by:
Trail Ahead Publishing
Woodstock, Georgia

Table of Contents with Checklist of Topics

Feel free to check off topics as your teen answers the question and masters the subject.

Introduction

It was a typical October day in my advanced marketing classroom. Students were busy working on their assignment to order new merchandise for the school store. One of my students, Jen, had gone into my adjacent office to use the school telephone. Minutes later she walked back into the room and announced loudly, "That company is out of business!"

"That can't be. I just called and ordered from them last week, Jen. What makes you say that?"

"I dialed the telephone number and got a message saying the call cannot be completed as dialed."

Jen explained that she tried three times and gestured to the number on the catalog in her hand. I chuckled, but the other teens in the group didn't see the humor or error.

Can you guess what occurred? Jen, being raised in a era of cell phones and having minimal use of a land line telephone, didn't know she had to dial a "1" BEFORE the long distance 10 digit number. When I explained, her eyes dropped to the floor. After all, she was an intelligent, college-bound senior in high school. How could she not know this information??? Simple. No one had taught her.

You are reading this book, so I know you are interested in helping future "Jens" of the world. As a parent, guardian, mentor, homeschooler, or someone who spends time with teenagers, you have the opportunity to utilize **L.I.F.E.** *(Learning Information For Everyday)* to ensure teens are taught the skills and information needed for an easier survival in everyday existence. This first book challenges basic knowledge and serves as a warm-up for future topics like communication, etiquette, money management, and employment. Adults should utilize the book with teens ages 13 to 19, although it's never too early to start building a solid foundation for adulthood.

As a 30 year educator in the private and public sector in several states, I developed an increasing awareness of situations like Jen's story. I taught a variety of courses including, but not exclusive to: marketing, fashion marketing, advanced marketing, entrepreneurship, business math, career exploration, and work-based-learning (also called work-exit or cooperative education) where students received school credit for working a job related to their career goal. Daily, I was bombarded with examples of *knowledge needed and wanted by teens* that was not in any class curriculum. Gaps in familiarity with concepts emerged during classes, in the halls, at student organization conferences, and during conversations and observations with adolescents ages 14-19. These gaps naturally related to my curriculum area as I was teaching business concepts while preparing students for careers and the world of work.

I am also a mother of two, Ben and Leah. Both are in their twenties now, and they too supplied material for these pages as my husband and I prepared them for independent living. Tom and I would engage them in various topics and questions during dinner or while driving long distances in the car. Once I started writing this book, I would question them to "test market" concepts herein and found, I too, had inadvertently failed to make sure they were versed on some of the information needed for everyday (having a book like this would have made our job a bit easier, methinks). In fact, we still have question- and-answer talks routinely. I feel pretty lucky in that regard.

Once retired from teaching, I wanted to share my discoveries and help others to challenge teenagers while reducing potential negative consequences for them in this complex world. Call it what you want... "common sense", "life skills", "basics". **You will be shocked to learn just what teenagers do not know.**

Don't expect lessons on sex, drugs, coping, emotional matters, and so on. There are abundant resources out there on those subjects. Instead, this book will alert you to things most adults learned a long time ago and never realized teenagers today do not know or utilize. It will be the **start of a dialogue to help facilitate a path to achievement** for teens. And you may even learn something new, get a refresher on something you had forgotten *or* learn something from that teen! (He/she knows a lot of things you don't. Just look at how advanced teens are in the technology field.)

It has been my experience, that despite an education system that spends millions of hours and dollars on testing youth before graduation, no school routinely tests LIFE skills such as household tasks, etiquette guidelines, community resource knowledge, how to get a job, and financial astuteness (to name a few). Instead, schools use "high-stakes testing" as a measure of graduation readiness. The media reports on test scores each year, but there is no mention of the ultimate measurement of our teens' success: **self-sufficiency through mastering knowledge needed to transition into and succeed in the adult world.** That is another motivation for writing this book and why mentors of teens will find this book helpful. You should appreciate an opportunity to do a *final teen graduation check/ test* before he/she enters the post-secondary life phase.

This "check/test" will have no calculus, questions about war heroes, questions about the great literary classics, and places no emphasis on the periodic table of elements. (The teens will be happy to hear this!) Instead, it is a "challenge" to see who has the knowledge and skills that will prevent anyone from being exploited, embarrassed, humiliated or the bearer of consequences for "just not knowing stuff" that is expected and allows learning or re-learning, as needed.

On this quest for answers, don't think that if your teen comes up empty on multiple questions in this book that you have failed as a parent or advisor ... *you have not!* As I have already admitted, my own children, who have been successful in both high school and college, could not answer many questions ... and I know *I'm not a bad parent!* (LOL — which means Laugh Out Loud, just in case you weren't sure!) I like to **think of the missing gaps as an *oversight* on our part. After all, we can't teach someone something, if we don't realize he/she doesn't know it!** (Did you follow that??? — Good!) Remember, there are many vocabulary words, terms, and acronyms that young people will hear, but may never ask their meaning, so adults *assume* they know it. (You'll see ... just wait!)

At the start of each new topic or chapter, you will find a numbered list of *questions, tasks, and/or vocabulary* to define that will challenge your teen's knowledge. Don't let this scare you, even if you can't answer some of the questions, I have supplied an *answer key* directly thereafter. (I am a teacher first, after all. You should have expected that!) And, although some answers could vary with ethnic, economic, or lifestyle differences, I stick to the middle ground in answering the questions and elaborating on the subject. I believe what is presented is the minimum you need to address to prevent teenagers from becoming overwhelmed, frustrated, and possibly in trouble in life. Feel free to add more in depth topics and questions and do research when applicable.

You will note that the questions are not multiple choice. Teens are really good guessers, weren't you? If you truly want to see what a teen knows, questions need to be *open-ended* ... increasing the likelihood of a good discussion and learning.

You can choose to read the **stories** or not. However, I expect you will enjoy and relate to these true stories. You may even find yourself chuckling as you acknowledge the scenario because you've witnessed something similar yourself (or can at least believe it to be so). The stories illustrate the need to be discussing the topic at hand and provide some levity.

Feel free to use the topics in any order or empower your teen to pick a topic of their choosing to start. You may give all the questions in one sitting, tackle one topic section at a time, or shuffle the questions. Consider having a "question of the day" to discuss over dinner, at the start of class or to end a meeting. All that matters is that we, as adults, are **asking the questions and preparing teenagers to be successful adults as they face life's challenges on their own.** (I'm not sure the old adage of "learning things the hard way" is really always necessary ... how about you?)

Don't forget to check out the **Let It Go** suggestion at the end of each chapter. These propose what we, as the older generation, may need to accept have changed for the 21st century. A "quit fighting a losing battle" suggestion for you and a consolation prize for teens who will be happy that you have modified your expectations in some areas.

You should find this book easy to use and read, as it is conversational and utilizes icons to earmark sections. Here is what each icon stands for:

QUESTIONS (topic questions to check for knowledge, skill and understanding)

ANSWER KEY (answers to the questions to clarify and assist)

TRUTH & CONSEQUENCES (rationale to explain why this topic is important)

NOTE (sideline pieces of information you may enjoy or find helpful)

TO DO (activities to check for know-how instead of oral responses)

STORY (true stories to illustrate need for topic at hand and for fun)

STEPS (list of steps to make learning a concept easier to follow)

DISCUSSION (this question will take true dialogue of give and take responses)

LET IT GO (suggestions for things that aren't worth the fight with this generation... helps you pick your battles and demonstrate a better understanding of the teen generation)

It is time to get started and I am pulling for the teens and hope they will get all the answers correct! Remember to treasure the time and chats with your adolescent(s) as you utilize the book. Embrace the unexpected laughs you share together as you journey through it!

TEST _ TEST _ TEST ...

THIS IS A TEST OF THE
EMERGENCY CHILD
REARING AGENCY.
THIS IS ONLY A TEST!

AND YOU NEED TO
GIVE IT TO A TEEN NOW!!

⑦ Warm-Up

1. What time is it?

 2. Find an analog clock. What time is it now?

3. If you have an appointment at 4:00 pm, in the United States, what time should you arrive to be "on-time"?

4. What is the measurement (in inches) indicated at the arrow point?

5. Calculate your current high school GPA (Grade Point Average)-what is it?

6. How do you write the following times using military time?

    a. 6:30 pm   b. 3:38 am   c. noon

7. Your best friend's grandmother just died. You want to attend the funeral. What will you wear?

8. COD stands for

    _____ _____ _____ Define COD.

<u>Misc. Vocab</u>-Define the following miscellaneous words:

9. Restitution

10. Want

11. Need

12. Jargon

13. Layman's Terms

⑨ Warm-Up

   Let's get started and see how your teenager(s) handle the warm-up questions. This is obviously a hodge-podge of topics to introduce the format in which you, the reader, can expect to enjoy the book hereafter. Good luck and enjoy!

 Let me remind you that each master topic will have a brief introduction. The "truth and consequences" section ⓣⓒ follows the introduction to provide a better understanding of why this topic is important for teens to know. The "question" will be presented again for your convenience, followed by the "answer or key" ⑨ for ease or if you are unsure yourself. Following most answers will be elaborations that are often needed to provide depth that the answer/key just does not provide. Here and there, "stories" ◕ bring real life illustration to the subject at hand. No doubt making you crack a smile or shake your head as you relate to the tale as it unfolds. The stories will also enable you to share with teenagers some examples of what has happened to others ... perhaps helping teens avoid the same thing down the road. This is when learning and practicing this L.I.F.E. knowledge or skill begins leading to success.

ⓣⓒ Each of the following warm-up questions have proven to give high school students trouble. (And not just a few students ... I would say many.) Although some of these topics were taught in elementary school, numerous teens struggle due to not using the skill consistently or never truly grasping the concept and transferring it to long term memory in the first place. So, this is the starting point for the Challenge...

Here's What Your Teen Needs To Know...

1. What time is it?

💡 1:51   6:24   12:39

With the new digital era, many young people stopped being able to read an analog (face) clock or watch. Why you ask? Because he/she has had little practice with the skill since learning it on worksheets in elementary school. Today, teens rely on cell phones to provide the time of day. They have become so accustomed to the abundance of digital clocks in society that analog time-telling has diminished. However, the face clock is still around and people need to be able to use it.

Since students were taught to tell time on a face clock prior to age 10, not having this skill as a teen is embarrassing. In my class, students would snicker and tease each other, but at least half of my students were unable to read a face clock. (That's fact... not an exaggeration!) I had to repeatedly deny student requests to check the time on their cell phone because cell phones weren't permitted to be used in my school (much like many job sites don't allow cell phone use). Some students had no choice but to check time on their cell phone which resulted in a 30 minute detention if caught. Let's change this, so teens aren't breaking rules, sneaking a peak or late due to the type of clock in a room.

Monica walked up to my teacher's desk asking to go to the restroom. I told her to "write a pass", and I'd sign it. (In the classroom, students had to write their own pass if they wanted to leave to go to the restroom, counselor's office, etc., and it had to include where they were heading and the time leaving.)

Monica wrote a pass with no time listed. When I asked why, she said, "I can't read that clock" and gestured to the analog clock on the wall. A group of nearby students busted out in laughter while Monica's face turned beet red. I gave the class one of my famous "looks" that settled them right down. I added the time to Monica's pass and sent her on her way. At the end of class, we had a quick review of time telling.

Here's a quick review:

→ Locate the shorter hand, which tells the hour. Here, the hour would be one o'clock because the short hand is between 1 and 2 (the hour is always the previous number).

→ Find the longer hand, which tells the minutes. Each of the 12 numbers on the face divides a 60 minute hour into 5 minute intervals. Beginning at 12, count 5 minutes for every time the long hand passes a bigger number. For example, 1 = :05 or 5 minutes and 8 = :40 or 40 minutes. In this example, the longer hand is just past the 50 minute mark.

→ Use the longer hand to find individual minutes between the 5 minute increments (some clocks even use hash marks to help you). For example, if the longer hand points between the 10 and 11 (like in the example), and is at the first marker to the right of the 10, then an additional minute (:01) is added. Hence, 50 + 1 or 51 minutes. If there are no markers, you must estimate the actual minute.

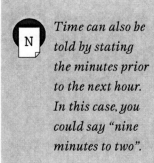

Time can also be told by stating the minutes prior to the next hour. In this case, you could say "nine minutes to two".

➥ Now read the time ... the hour first, followed by the minutes. The time is 1:51.

 2. Find an analog clock. What time is it now?

3. If you have an appointment at 4:00 pm, in the United States, what time should you arrive to be "on-time"?

As a rule, 3:50 pm

Tom was interviewing Jeff for a sales position. The interview time was 8:00 am, so Tom arrived at the office early (about 7:30 am that day). When Jeff finally arrived, it was 8:28. Jeff claimed he got lost, but Tom didn't care. He refused to interview him and sent him away.

Jeff should have driven the route before the interview to ensure that he knew where he was going and should have called when he knew he was going to be late. Would you want to waste your time waiting for someone who is late? Would you trust Jeff to be on time for client calls or for work each morning?

To be "on-time" in the U.S. a person typically arrives ten minutes early, although there may be exceptions. Coming sooner than that can be awkward and put the person you are meeting under pressure to "hurry up" because you are waiting for them. Arriving ten minutes early shows that you care enough to be prompt without adding undue pressure. Never be late to an appointment, but if something happens, call to alert and apologize as soon as possible.

Here are more guidelines for specific events:

Dinner Party — on time and up to 15-30 minutes late
Job Interview — 10 minutes early
Show or Movie — 5-10 minutes before show time
Wedding — 10-15 minutes early

4. What is the measurement (in inches) indicated at the arrow point?

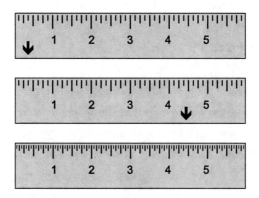

Ⓠ 3 and 1/2 inch; 3/8 inch; 4 and 7/16 inch

📓 *Johnny had just been hired to do part-time work helping his neighbor build decks for the summer. The first day, the boss shared the blue-prints for the deck and asked him to cut the 2 X 12 pieces of lumber to the correct length for the outside frame. Johnny needed four boards, each cut to 10 3/16. He got his tape measure, guessed at the 3/16 mark, and cut. When the boss re-measured Johnny's work, he called him over to ask why the length wasn't right.*

Johnny had the cost of four wasted boards deducted from his paycheck, had to spend time re-cutting new boards, and had the boss questioning his ability level because he was forced to guess his ruler measurements. Made for a rough day and lesson at the age of 17.

Consequences for "guessing", wasting materials, and not asking for help can have a wide range of outcomes in the workplace, but losing money is at the top of the list on "no-no's". I am happy to report that measuring and reading a ruler using whole inches is a solid skill of teens today. Competency using quarters, halves, three-fourths is fairly solid. However, the majority have forgotten what they learned in grade school on how to read eighths and sixteenths on a ruler. (Don't ask the skill level for measuring to the thirty-seconds mark or reading a metric ruler ... please!)

Some would say, if you don't do construction work, you don't need this skill. I disagree. What about general life use? Wouldn't you use a ruler when hanging a picture, measuring for blinds or carpet, checking space needed for a new refrigerator, or doing an art project? (Let's be practical and make sure our teens can use a ruler properly.)

To review, remind your teen that each inch is most commonly divided into 16 parts (but can be marked in 32rds, so beware).

 ➥ Find the whole inch needed.

➥ Count the number of hash marks past the whole inch mark/ number to find the fractional part.

Ex: if you need 2 and 3/16 inch, count 3 hash marks past the 2 inch mark (as indicated by the arrow on page 16) assuming the ruler is divided by 16ths

5. Calculate your current high school GPA (Grade Point Average) - what is it?

 Answers will vary

Kacy was sitting in her senior homeroom crying because Ms. Selden had just taught the group how to calculate their high school GPA (Grade Point Average).

"1.4 GPA! That won't get me into Kennesaw University!" Kacy screamed.

"Now Kacy, remember that colleges base admission on extra-curricular activities, SAT, ACT, and GPA scores", Ms. Selden calmly stated as she walked towards the distraught student. She knew Kacy was devastated to find out that her post-secondary plan wasn't realistic. Ms. Selden kept thinking that had Kacy known how to calculate her GPA to get an idea of her standing in regards to entrance expectations for a college, she could have prepared more realistically.

"Didn't anyone ever teach you this?"

"No!" Kacy said between sniffles. "I know I had a few low grades here and there, but I took a few failed classes over. Doesn't that help? No college will want me with this GPA!"

Don't let this happen to your teen! Data and reality are good things! There are careers that require four or more years of formal education and some as little as six months after high school. Also, there are careers that train a person while on-the-job. All these careers have value, but require different preparation for employment.

We all can't be surgeons, engineers or chief executive officers (CEO) and not everyone would want to be. (Thank goodness!)

Help teens develop a realistic view of his or her future and what is required to achieve that dream. If she truly wants to be a surgeon, then *make sure she knows early what her GPA is* and what universities will *require* in a GPA for her to pursue her career passion. Encourage her to research online, talk to people in the industry, and even consult a school counselor (they tend to know more about post-secondary options than we do). Discuss the level of dedication associated with your teen's quest and determine if the ability level is really there. (And remind teens that the GPA is just one part of the career equation for attending colleges and universities. Activities, leadership, and course selections also will be considered.) Don't forget that financial capabilities must also enter into the equation.

What's important *is to help guide your teen to a practical career path.* If, for example, the teen you are working with doesn't have the grades to be a surgeon, then suggest becoming a surgical technician/assistant. This will take 9-24 months of training from a community or technical college and is a more realistic goal. That's being a good parent or mentor! You aren't killing anyone's dream (never talk a young person out of their dreams) ... you are **helping to shape a successful dream!**

Adolescents who don't connect high school grades, coursework taken, and class rigor to career path options available after graduation, tend to flounder and have delays in starting life as an independent adult. My observation, after 30-years teaching, is that unrealistic "career pipe dreams" lead to more post-secondary school dropouts, job hopping, student (and adult) frustration, and the real possibility that individuals will still be living in their parent's house (or basement) at age 28. Assuming that's not your vision or theirs, now is the time to alter the path by having open and honest discussions concerning high school GPA.

Calculating GPA Guidelines

Assuming the school system is using the most common 4 point scale with semester grading, look at the transcript and transcribe accordingly:

GPA 4 Point Scale

Grade	% grade	Points
A	90-100%	4
B	80-90%	3
C	71-79%	2
D	70%	1
F	0-69%	0

Example Transcript Transcription for 9th grader after one semester completed

Course Taken	Semester Grade	Semester Point Scale
9th Lit/Comp A	90	4
Algebra 1 A	75	2
Health	83	3
Biology	65	0
Geography	70	1
Band	95	4

Now figure out the average by counting up the grades and averaging:

# of grades of 90-100 = __ × 4 = __	2 × 4 = 8
# of grades of 80-89 = __ × 3 = __	1 × 3 = 3
# of grades of 71-79 = __ × 2 = __	1 × 2 = 2
# of grades of 70 = __ × 1 = __	1 × 1 = 1
# of grades of 0-69 = __ × 0 = __	1 × 0 = 0

14 points in total

Total Number of Points = _____
        divided by total # of classes __

        = __ GPA

14 points divided by 6 classes
        = 2.33 GPA

6. How do you write the following times using military time?

    a. 6:30 pm → 1830 hours
    b. 3:38 am → 0338 hours
    c. noon → 1200 hours

Because military time is the prevalent method for stating time of day across the world, teens need to know both standard time and be able to do the conversion to military time.

N *Students must include an "F" grade & calculate the zero into the formula. Additionally, if a student has a 1 credit course (instead of a .5) because of block scheduling or a 2 period lab-type class, the grade counts twice, so count it as 2 classes. AP (Advanced Placement) credit is NOT addressed here. See a school counselor for help with AP coursework calculations.*

Here are the steps to help write military time:

➥ Know that the military clock starts at midnight. Midnight is called "Zero Hundred Hours" (0000 hours) and runs consecutively for twenty-four hours, not twelve. Hours are written without a colon.

➥ Hours from midnight to noon, you add a zero before the hour and two zeros (or the number of minutes) afterward. For example, 2 am is 0200 hours. 10:12 am is 1012 hours.

➥ Hours from noon to midnight, you continue to count beyond 1200 for each passing hour (1300, 1400, 1500, etc.) and add two zeros (or the number of minutes) afterward. For example, 6 pm is 1800 hours. 11:49 pm is 2349 hours.

To say hours in military time:

➥ If there is a zero as the first digit, say the "zero" and the number followed by "hundred hours" (0200 hours is pronounced "zero two hundred hours")

➥ If there is a one or two as the first digit, say the first two numbers as a pair of numbers (1100 hours is "eleven hundred hours")

➥ If there are hours and minutes involved, say the four digit number as two pairs of numbers (1830 hours is "eighteen thirty hours" or 0338 hours is "zero three thirty-eight hours)

Using the word "hours" is optional. Saying "oh" (instead of "zero") as the first digit, is acceptable for civilian use. Ex: oh-800 would be 8 o'clock.

Remember midnight to noon reads a time that is less than 1200 hours and noon to midnight is time more than 1200 hours. The first two digits in military time give the hour and the second two digits give the minutes with NO colon in between.

Helpful Hints for Learning Military Time

- Hours from 1 am to noon are the same as civilian time.
- Hours from 1 pm to midnight, subtract 1200 to get standard time or add 1200 to get military time.
- When saying military time, numbers are said as a "hundred", not "thousands".
- Using military time eliminates the confusion between am and pm.

Military to Civilian	Military to Civilian
0001 = 12:01 am	1300 = 1:00 pm
0100 = 1:00 am	1400 = 2:00 pm
0200 = 2:00 am	1500 = 3:00 pm
0300 = 3:00 am	1600 = 4:00 pm
0400 = 4:00 am	1700 = 5:00 pm
0500 = 5:00 am	1800 = 6:00 pm
0600 = 6:00 am	1900 = 7:00 pm
0700 = 7:00 am	2000 = 8:00 pm
0800 = 8:00 am	2100 = 9:00 pm
0900 = 9:00 am	2200 = 10:00 pm
1000 = 10:00 am	2300 = 11:00 pm
1100 = 11:00 am	2400 = 12 midnight
1200 = noon	

7. Your best friend's grandmother just died. You want to attend the funeral. What will you wear?

(?) Males should wear conservative dress slacks, a button-up shirt, socks, belt, and dress shoes at a minimum-Females should wear a conservative dress (not too tight, short, or low-cut) or dress pants and top (blouse or sweater), and dress shoes

N *Religious preferences and cultural traditions may demand alterations to the customary attire described within, so tell teens to do their homework before dressing for a funeral. Also, know that if the deceased is a member of your family, attire tends to be of a more "dressed-up" nature as you are the host/hostess of the event and are setting the standard.*

It is just appalling that so many individuals today will not take the time and effort required to dress nicely to pay their last respects to the deceased and his/her family (and it's not just teens). Wearing jeans, a t-shirt, and tattered clothing at a graveside is a bold statement that someone just doesn't care or doesn't know any better.

History had us all wearing very conservative, black attire to funerals. In fact, both men and women typically had a "funeral outfit" that they kept strictly for this occasion. Today, it is acceptable to wear colors other than black, but discretion needs to be applied. A bold, flowered print dress or Mickey Mouse tie is still not appropriate. Men can usually skip the tie and suit coat if just stopping to pay respects at the funeral home, but should consider wearing one to the actual burial service (especially if held in a church or chapel). Women should apply the same logic to their garments.

8. COD stands for

_____ _____ _____ Define COD.

> **CASH ON DELIVERY**-Providing cash payment at the time merchandise is received from a delivery carrier

Once a person provides payment for a delivered item, he/she will be allowed to take possession of the item. For example, when a person gets pizza delivered, he/she must provide the pizza driver with cash if you want him/her to hand over the pizza box. In the world today, COD is used less and less as we have become a "plastic" society that uses credit cards and credit accounts in lieu of cash. However, in the business world, COD is still used on occasion and should be a familiar term.

9. Restitution

> Making amends for the loss, damage, or injury that one caused-this involves paying for a replacement, repairing an item, or compensating in some way that is equivalent to the loss felt by the inflicted party

The day before the high school band had to march in the Chicago parade, the whole group got to visit the Navy Pier and do some sightseeing. The band director gave his normal speech about being representatives of the school and conducting themselves appropriately. The students had all heard the speech before, but knew to nod their heads before running towards the amusement rides, smiling. Approximately an hour later, the band director's phone rang and he was called to the Pier's security office.

Upon entering the office, he saw Caleb, Katie, Cam, and Amanda. Katie, the only freshman in the group, was crying uncontrollably. Mr. Harris directed his attention to the officer who had already started to explain that these four students were caught on security cameras defacing the Ferris wheel by writing their names on the inside of the car. Katie was the one with the marker in her hand and was told she would have to pay "restitution" and possibly face criminal charges.

Needless to say, Katie didn't get much sleep that night and it was a long bus ride home for these partners in crime. Katie had no idea what restitution meant and she was fearful. Restitution sounded so serious to her, when in actuality, restitution was the lightest sentence/consequence offered by the court for her actions. Katie should have been feeling relieved, instead of sick to her stomach (although she still had her parents to face).

10. **Want**

 The lack of something desired

11. **Need**

 Something required to survive (food, shelter, clothing and water)

"Mommy, I really NEED a new pair of jeans!!!" How many times has a teen announced that one? Are you chuckling to yourself as you know most teen's closets and drawers are overflowing and there is no risk of he/she being naked tomorrow at school?

It is important that young people know that a need is a true necessity and a want is just a longing or craving for something. Although these words are often used interchangeably, they are not

the same thing and people should strive to use the terms correctly in personal and business situations.

12. **Jargon**

 Language used within a particular culture or profession

Jargon is wording and terminology used within a group or industry as a common language of discussion. Think of jargon as wording used by a professional or expert in a field.

13. **Layman's Terms**

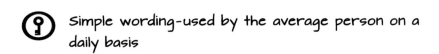 Simple wording-used by the average person on a daily basis

The average person uses "layman's terms" when describing something because he/she is not typically familiar with the technical terms referred to as jargon.

That's the warm-up section. A hodgepodge of possibly missing knowledge and skills in the teenager(s) you deal with regularly. As you continue to the home life section, remember that more information on any and all topics discussed in this book can be found by researching on the internet, in the library or by talking with others. The goal within these pages is to broadly introduce topics of importance for teens so you can help them start the quest to improve themselves and prepare to be the best they can be in the world!

Don't expect watches to be worn daily by this generation as they use their cell phones for telling time. Watches will be worn as a fashion accessory to enhance an outfit or worn strictly on special occasions. Watches aren't used to tell time by teens these days, so LET IT GO!

⑦ Home Life

1. What is the first thing you should do if the toilet is overflowing?

2. Have your teen *demonstrate* the following tasks related to Minor Home Repairs:
   - ☐ use a hammer to pound in a nail
   - ☐ use a drill
   - ☐ hang a picture in drywall/plaster using an anchor bolt
   - ☐ hang a picture into a wall stud
   - ☐ change the filter in the furnace/air conditioning unit
   - ☐ test the smoke alarm
   - ☐ patch a hole in drywall
   - ☐ paint and trim a wall in a room
   - ☐ use a hand saw to cut a board in half or cut a limb off a tree outside

3. What is the best way to put out a grease fire on the kitchen stove?

<u>Misc. Vocab</u>-Define the following cooking related words...

4. Whisk

5. Dice

6. Chop

7. Mix

8. Stir

9. Blanch

10. Al dente

11. Freezer Burn

What do the following cooking abbreviations stand for?

12. T

13. t

14. oz.

15. lb.

16. c

17. pt.

18. qt.

19. gal.

20. Have your teen *demonstrate* the following tasks related to Cooking:

- ☐ plan and create a meal using fresh food from all four food groups (no pre-packed foods allowed)
- ☐ follow a recipe and make a meal
- ☐ defrost the freezer (if your freezer is automatic defrost, just discuss how to safely defrost a freezer that is not ... like a dormatory refrigerator would be)
- ☐ identify freezer burn on an item
- ☐ check for expiration date on five items in the cupboard or pantry

21. Why do you sometimes find buttons sewn into the inside of a new shirt?

 22. Have your teen *demonstrate* the following tasks related to General Home Life:

- ☐ iron a shirt
- ☐ sew on a button
- ☐ hem a pair of pants
- ☐ mend a clothing hole
- ☐ do a load of laundry
- ☐ empty lint filter on dryer
- ☐ dust a room
- ☐ make a bed
- ☐ clean a window (without smears)
- ☐ effectively pack a suitcase
- ☐ vacuum a room
- ☐ fold a fitted sheet
- ☐ load and run dishwasher

☐ use a plunger
☐ sweep with a broom
☐ locate main power breaker in your living quarters
☐ locate main water shut-off valve in your living quarters
☐ reset breaker after a loss of power in an area of your living quarters

23. Can you list all the medication(s) you take daily? (include name, purpose, dosage, possible side effects and doctor)

24. What is the full name and telephone number of your doctor?

25. What is the name of your medical insurance company?

26. What is a medical insurance card?

27. Where is your medical insurance card? Why do you need one?

28. What is the difference between the group number and member identification number on a medical insurance card?

29. What does EOB mean, related to health or medical insurance?

30. Share an *EOB statement* with your teenager and let them see the information held within.

31. What is the medical history of your family (heart disease, cancer, arthritis, diabetes, stroke, etc.) and what relative (mom, dad, maternal grandmother/father or paternal grandmother/father) has/had the disease or condition and who died (especially at an early age) from that medical condition?

32. List what is in your wallet currently. (Be specific like the company name on each credit card)

33. What is your social security number?

34. Have your teen *demonstrate* the following tasks related to Car Maintenance:
- ☐ change a tire
- ☐ check tire pressure
- ☐ fill car with gas & pay
- ☐ add wiper fluid
- ☐ check transmission fluid (check when engine is hot)
- ☐ check car oil (check when engine is cold)
- ☐ add oil if needed or demonstrate how to add
- ☐ change car wiper blades
- ☐ jump a dead car battery with cables (or simulate)

⑨ Home Life

The most important parental and adulthood duty we have after providing the basics of food, shelter, and clothing for our youth, is to educate them. (Don't you agree?) This involves more than supporting their efforts at the local school or post-secondary institution. And as much as we all love having children and teenagers in the house (at least most of the time), it is crucial to teach what they need to know, so he/she *can move out and be independent, productive, self-supporting adults*. The Home Life section covers what may seem trivial, but remember that *the goal is to check* that the simplest things in life haven't been overlooked in our teachings.

TC Regardless of family net worth or circumstance, teens need know-how to take care of themselves in a home, apartment, or dorm. Ask yourself if the teenagers you know have used a drill and screwdriver, cleaned the house, dealt with a stuffed toilet, done the laundry or been introduced to medical insurance. I actually had a teen tell me that "My parents have someone who does that for us, so I don't have to know how to do it." (Must be nice, huh?)

I have found that many American households have evolved to where chores traditionally done by the family are routinely "outsourced" (hired out) now. (I'm guilty of some of that myself.) As a result, adults have to question whether teens *could do* the basic home tasks once living on their own. Afterall, young adults typically aren't able to afford to have the same services done for them as the adults they know who have years of work experience resulting in elevated salaries. They will start out making an entry-level wage and will probably have little money saved. *Outsourcing is expensive*! Therefore,

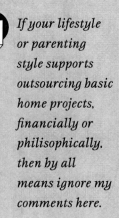

we need to avoid having our young adults living in a dirty apartment, calling every time something breaks, or getting instructions on how to make a simple meal. (Remember the *independent adult* thing I discussed earlier?) Independence doesn't exist when the apron string or phone cord is still attached on *a daily basis*. What if times get rough down the line and our young adults need to "cut-back" on hired out services? Can he/she do the chore themselves? Can he/she teach their own children how to be self-sufficient?

N *If your lifestyle or parenting style supports outsourcing basic home projects, financially or philisophically, then by all means ignore my comments here.*

Everyone needs home survival skills, so teach them the basics.

Here's What Your Teen Needs To Know ...

1. What is the first thing you should do if the toilet is overflowing?

   Turn off the water valve (located behind the toilet and close to the floor)

You can laugh all you want, but many teens (and some adults — let's be truthful) will stand over an overflowing toilet yelling (with profanity at times), frantically grabbing for towels, while the water keeps coming over the top of the bowl. In actuality, squatting down to see behind the toilet, grabbing the valve behind the toilet base, and turning off the water flow is all it takes to save the day (remember ... righty, tighty ... lefty, loosey).

2. Have your teen *demonstrate* the following tasks related to Minor Home Repairs:
   - ☐ use a hammer to pound in a nail
   - ☐ use a drill
   - ☐ hang a picture in drywall/plaster using an anchor bolt
   - ☐ hang a picture into a wall stud
   - ☐ change the filter in the furnace/air conditioning unit
   - ☐ test the smoke alarm
   - ☐ patch a hole in drywall
   - ☐ paint and trim a wall in a room
   - ☐ use a hand saw to cut a board in half or cut a limb off a tree outside

David was working with a group of junior and senior teens from his church on a Habitat for Humanity house project. Despite the 90 degree Georgia temperatures, the teens were all eager to help the 81-year old widow get her house like new again. The boys on the crew showed up promptly at 7 o'clock in the morning and David quickly assigned each of them a different task.

After the rest of the crew arrived and were put to work, David walked around the worksite to check on each teen and inspect their work. As David approached Liam, he noticed Liam was holding the hammer about 2 inches back from the claw head instead of at the end of the handle. He was taking short, little strokes, and barely making progress towards getting the nail in place.

After a quick disguised smirk, David asked Liam if he had ever done any work like this before and offered him a lesson on a more efficient way to swing a hammer. David explained that holding the handle down further on the handle allowed the leverage needed to hammer that nail in like a bullet. Liam watched the demonstration with shock and intrigue before taking over to finish the job.

3. What is the best way to put out a grease fire on the kitchen stove?

🔢 Turn off the heat, cover the pot with a metal lid, and pour lots of baking soda on top of the flames-if the fire is big and caused from a flammable liquid or gas, use a Class B Dry Chemical Fire Extinguisher

Remind your teen that fire is nothing to mess with! If the situation seems to be getting out of control, he/she needs to get out and call 911. (If the fire is spreading, the smoke is increasing, or the methods to extinguish the fire aren't working, then it is out of control.) However, often a person can manage the situation by remembering a few easy rules:

1. Never try to move the pot/pan that is on fire.
2. Never use a glass lid to cover the pot/pan as the extreme heat could make it shatter (a cookie sheet works great).
3. NEVER USE WATER. Water on a grease fire will go below the flames and allow the oil to continue burning. The water can convert to steam and

Fire alarm batteries should be changed every six months. Get into the habit of changing the batteries when you change your clocks for Daylight Savings time. Also check your fire extinguisher in the spring and fall as part of the Daylight Savings time routine.

splash (or explode) burning oil into the air and spread the

fire. If it is an electrical fire, electricity will travel through the water and intensify the problem, so avoid water.

4. Do not use flour, use *baking soda*. Even though flour looks like baking soda, it is flammable and possibly explosive. Salt can help absorb the grease if used *with* the baking soda.

5. Use a Class B Dry Chemical Fire Extinguisher if the fire is caused by cooking liquids (oil or grease). These extinguishers release a cloud of carbon dioxide that will smother the fire. Class B extinguishers are used for flammable liquids, oils, greases, tars, oil-based paints, flammable gases, and every kitchen needs one. Most look like this and can be identified by the "B" on the label:[1]

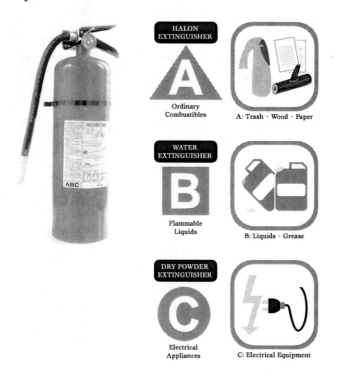

HALON
EXTINGUISHER

A

Ordinary
Combustibles

A: Trash · Wood · Paper

WATER
EXTINGUISHER

B

Flammable
Liquids

B: Liquids · Grease

DRY POWDER
EXTINGUISHER

C

Electrical
Appliances

C: Electrical Equipment

ABC

1 http://www.wikihow.com/Put-out-a-Grease-Fire

Fire extinguishers often are manufactured for "mixed" uses and will have the A, B, and C class ratings. The following tells you what type of fire the different classes are effective against...

"Class A" are for paper, wood, textiles and plastics.

"Class B" are for flammable liquids (cooking liquids, oil, gas, kerosene or paint).

"Class C" are for electrical equipment.

Since tank sizes differ, they will also contain a number (sometimes in front of the A, B or C) that indicate the rating size of fire the unit can extinguish. For more detailed information, read your extinguisher directions, research online, at the library or with your local fire department.

MAKE SURE YOU CHECK YOUR FIRE EXTINGUISHER REGULARLY TO ENSURE IT HAS A CHARGE AND DOESN'T NEED MAINTENANCE

To use a fire extinguisher:

- Hold by the handle with nozzle pointing away from you and pull the pin, located below the trigger.
- Stand up to 10 feet away from the fire.
- Point the extinguisher discharge horn/hose at the base of the fire and keep canister upright.
- Starting at the front edge, squeeze the trigger slowly and expel the dry chemical evenly sweeping the hose from side to side.[2]
- Continue until fire is out.

---

2 http://www.wikihow.com/Use-a-Fire-Extinguisher

Misc. Vocab-Define the following cooking related words ...

4. Whisk

   🔑 to move quickly with sweeping strokes of rapid movements (also called whipping)

5. Dice

   🔑 cut into small cubes

6. Chop

   🔑 cut into small pieces

7. Mix

   🔑 to combine or join together with or without a tool (typically using an electric mixer)

8. Stir

   🔑 join together in repeated motion to combine (typically by hand with a spoon)

9. Blanch

   🔑 to scald briefly with boiling water, then drain (also known as parboiling)

10. Al dente

   🔑 cook without being soft; still firm to the bite (used for cooking pasta)

11. Freezer Burn

   🔑 grayish-brown spots that appear on frozen food when air reaches the food and starts to dry it out due to improper or poor packaging

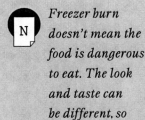

Freezer burn doesn't mean the food is dangerous to eat. The look and taste can be different, so forewarn teens.

What do the following cooking abbreviations stand for?

12. T

   🔑 tablespoon

13. t

   🔑 teaspoon

14. oz.

   🔑 ounce

15. lb.

   🔑 pound

16. c

   🔑 cup

17. pt.

   🔑 pint

18. qt.

   🔑 quart

19. gal.

   🔑 gallon

20. Have your teen *demonstrate* the following tasks related to Cooking:

- ☐ plan and create a meal using fresh food from all four food groups (no pre-packed foods allowed)
- ☐ follow a recipe and make a meal
- ☐ defrost the freezer (if your freezer is automatic defrost, just discuss how to safely defrost a freezer that is not...like a dormatory refrigerator would be)
- ☐ identify freezer burn on an item
- ☐ check for expiration date on five items in the cupboard or pantry

Take a moment and discuss the difference between the terms "sell by", "use by", and "best by" which are stamped on many food and over-the-counter medicine products. Most likely the distinction between these will not be life threatening, but they sure could make a difference in whether your teen has a distasteful eating experience, an upset stomach or gets no relief from a pending ailment. Tell your teen that items that require refrigeration have a shorter life after the expiration date than canned goods. "Best Used By:" and "Sell By:" mean just what they say, so that's easy.

Some of you are reading this and thinking that you don't cook yourself, so there is no one to model this skill. My response is to take this opportunity to learn together or find some help. I promise you will have some real laughs in the process! Even now, I find myself smiling as I think back to the days when my kids were learning to cook and flour was all over the countertop, floor, and our clothing. Or when my niece had her whole arm stuck inside a 25 pound turkey as she prepared it for Thanksgiving dinner. Gotta savor those memories!

21. **Why do you sometimes find buttons sewn into the inside of a new shirt?**

❓ **These are replacement buttons for the shirt**

Often buttons are made with unique patterns, logos, designs, colors or textures that enhance the details of a garment. Since you would not be able to purchase a replica at the local discount, craft or fabric store, better manufacturers provide customers with extra buttons in the event one is lost.

 22. **Have your teen *demonstrate* the following tasks related to General Home Life:**
- ☐ iron a shirt
- ☐ sew on a button
- ☐ hem a pair of pants
- ☐ mend a clothing hole
- ☐ do a load of laundry
- ☐ empty lint filter on dryer
- ☐ dust a room
- ☐ make a bed
- ☐ clean a window *(without smears)*
- ☐ effectively pack a suitcase
- ☐ vacuum a room
- ☐ fold a fitted sheet
- ☐ load and run dishwasher
- ☐ use a plunger
- ☐ sweep with a broom

☐ locate main power breaker in your
living quarters
☐ locate main water shut-off valve in your
living quarters
☐ reset breaker after a loss of power in an
area of your living quarters

23. Can you list all the medication(s) you take daily? (include
name, purpose, dosage, possible side effects
and doctor)

 Answers will vary

*Be aware of
expiration dates
and refill deadlines
on prescriptions.*

Hopefully, all individuals, not just
teens, have a clear grasp of the medications
he/she takes, but please be sure. Do not
let your teenager *just* give you the color,
shape or size of the pill when answering
this question. (You know … a reply like
"I take that little, round, pink pill in the mornings.") He/she needs
to know the color, shape and size of the pill *and* the medical name
and dosage.

Remind your teen that different doses, manufacturers, or phar-
mancies *may* change the size, shape, and color of pills. Therefore,
don't hesitate to ask the pharmacist and make sure the correct medication was dispensed. Discuss generic brands vs. name brand products.
Explain how generics have a similar composition, are less expensive,
and will have a name that is different from a name brand medicaton
that a doctor prescribed. The rule of thumb is to "Be Alert!"

Discuss openly and honestly what the medical diagnosis is that
requires a certain medicine. Don't provide your teen with a watered

down version like "this is a concentration medicine". If he has ADD (Attention Deficit Disorder), use that terminology. Make sure medication side effects are discussed. Young people think they are invincible (we thought we were in our youth) and will tend to ignore issues for too long of a period. And while you are having a discussion, include the risk(s) in selling prescription drugs. Not only is it against the law and dangerous, it is contributing to the fastest growing drug problem of this century and needs to be addressed at home, in schools, and in the general public.

Make sure teenagers know the medications you take, as a parent or guardian. I suggest putting together a list of all the family members and their medication, doses, diagnosis, etc. and store it somewhere convenient. This can be a life saving measure in an emergency.

24. What is the full name and telephone number of your doctor?

Answers will vary

25. What is the name of your medical insurance company?

Answers will vary

26. What is a medical insurance card?

A travel size form/card (size of a credit card) that details pertinent information for an individual that proves medical insurance coverage and benefits exist

27. Where is your medical insurance card? Why do you need one?

Answers will vary but in a wallet would be a great response-a person needs a medical insurance card to avoid paying full price and/or cash at a medical facility and to avoid the possibility of being denied treatment at certain establishments

Remind your teen that medical facilities often require photo identification in addition to an insurance card before providing services. However, a medical facility does not need your social security number and you should not share it, even though many forms may ask.

Without proof of medical insurance via this card, medical facilities could require cash on the spot. In addition, some facilities won't take you as a patient without insurance and identification. When teenagers start going to the doctor and answering medical questions by themselves (if they haven't started already), knowledge of medication, insurance, allergies, and family medical history is important to ensure the best medical care. So, quiz your teen to ensure he/she has this information covered. (Adults are not always available when this information is needed ... after all, grown-ups have a life to live too!)

It is suggested that *teens carry his/her own insurance card*. Additional cards can be requested by calling the insurance company or requesting one through the insurance company's website. Most companies now allow temporary extra copies to be printed from their website.

Jackie's parents were out of town when she woke up on Saturday morning feeling like she couldn't breathe and was "coughing up a lung". She didn't want to worry her parents, as they needed this escape weekend, so she decided to go to the local Emergency Medical Clinic (after talking to her best friend for advice). Since she had never been to any doctor without her mom, she was feeling unsure and intimidated as she opened the door. After pausing, she mustered up the courage to approach the counter and speak to the receptionist. Jackie was asked to sign-in and was handed seven pages of forms on a clipboard. Just before she turned to walk away, the clerical nurse asked for proof of insurance. Jackie stopped short. She looked at the receptionist with confusion and fear. Now Jackie was crying, coughing, and wheezing!

28. What is the difference between the group number and member identification number on a medical insurance card?

(?) The group number is a unique number that identifies the company or plan within the insurance offered - the member identification number is specific to a policy holder who is carrying the insurance under an employer's company plan or through an outside group or government program

Review the insurance card with your teen making sure he/she knows the name of the insurance company that insures them. Point out that the "member ID" (or identification number) is assigned to a *specific individual* (policy holder and their dependents) *who has requested the insurance*. This person typically has their name listed on the card (i.e., Jane Doe). Health care providers use this number to confirm the coverage and benefits for an individual. This number

Can your teen tell you where to find his/her parent or guardian's will, health directives, insurance papers and banking documents in case of an emergency? Do they know who to ask if he/she needs help (executor, trustee, aunt/uncle, etc.) in the event that something happens to their parent or guardian? They need this information even though there's a 95% chance they will never need it.

will be different from the "group number". A medical facility may ask for the ID number and/or group number.

The group number identifies the company or insurance group (i.e., XYZ Company/Group). If the insurance coverage is through an employer, make sure the teen knows which parent (person or organization) "carries" the insurance (also called subscriber name) and the name of the company providing insurance coverage. (Don't laugh, I have asked many students where their parent works and they say "I don't know!") Point out that all cards do not look alike and the insurance company address and telephone numbers may be on the back.

Don't forget to explain what a "co-pay" is, even if you personally don't have one. Insurance plans and providers change throughout life and he/she may need to know this at some point.

29. What does EOB mean, related to health or medical insurance?

 Explanation of Benefits

Explanation of Benefits is exactly what it sounds like … this is the document that *explains* what medical procedures have been covered by the *insurance benefits*. This is the report that one will access to compare what part of a medical bill the insurance company discounted, paid, and what part is left to be paid by the subscriber. If you dare ... you can get into deductibles, in-network, out-of-network, adjustments, etc. Just don't overwhelm teens. Insurance is pretty complicated and boring for adults to digest, so think of it from a younger point of view as you talk.

 30. Share an EOB statement with your teenager and let them see the information held within.

31. What is the medical history of your family (heart disease, cancer, arthritis, diabetes, stroke, etc.) and what relative (mom, dad, maternal grandmother/father or paternal grandmother/father) has/had the disease or condition, and who died (especially at an early age) from that medical condition?.

(?) Answers will vary

Go back two generations (parents and grandparents) and discuss family medical history. (Think of this as a good time to review the family tree!) *This history is vertical, up the family tree so to speak. It does not include cousins or aunts and uncles.* Make sure teens can tie the medical issue to a particular person, as most new patient inquiries will want to know how this person is/was related to your teen. And while you are at it, allow everyone to share a few funny family stories or unique family facts. For example, my grandmother was one of twenty-one children. How wild is that? Sharing makes this discussion a lot more fun and less of a chore.

32. **List what is in your wallet currently.** (Be specific like the company name on each credit card)

 Answers will vary

The amount of money isn't the crucial thing, although teens may feel that way. It is important that he/she knows what is in their wallet in case it is stolen or misplaced. A list of debit and credit cards (and the account numbers), insurance cards, work/school identification cards, and the like, is what you need to see when you compare the list to the wallet. Making a photo copy of the important items is an easy way to keep a record of contents for the future. (Remember not to judge what random things a young person deems important to carry within his/her wallet.)

Suggest to your teen that he/she keep their wallet in the same place each day. Mention that a stolen wallet makes one an easy target for identity theft and is a painstaking occurrence to resolve, so be aware of its location at all times. Never keep passwords, bank account numbers, or a social security card in a wallet and carry only what is needed.

33. **What is your social security number?**

 Answers will vary - just make sure it has 9-digits

Again, remind your adolescent not to carry a social security card on his/her person daily. Encourage your teen to memorize the number and keep the physical card in a safety deposit box at the bank, in a home safe, or at a minimum, in a file drawer with other important documents.

34. Have your teen *demonstrate* the following tasks related to Car Maintenance:

- ☐ change a tire
- ☐ check tire pressure
- ☐ fill car with gas & pay
- ☐ add wiper fluid
- ☐ check transmission fluid (check when engine is hot)
- ☐ check car oil (check when engine is cold)
- ☐ add oil if needed or demonstrate how to add
- ☐ change car wiper blades
- ☐ jump a dead car battery with cables (or simulate)

Don't forget to make sure your teen knows how to wash a car too! I was amazed at how many teens don't realize one has to rinse the car first, then soap it, and finish with a rinse. Go over tire/rim cleaning and window cleaning. And funny as this may sound, review that rinsing and scrubbing from the roof down is the way to go. Otherwise, the dirt will roll down over the clean areas and many don't think about that when doing this task!

When Donnie got to Emma's house for their date, he announced that they would need to stay in tonight and just watch television. Mrs. West asked why when she overhead this conversation. Donnie told her he was low on gas in his car. Mrs. West crinkled her nose not understanding any of this. Finally, she asked Donnie if he had money to buy gasoline.

"Sure, I do", he said.

"Well then, what's the problem?"

With eyes to the floor and pink cheeks, Donnie explained to Emma's mother that his dad always filled his tank with gas. Donnie's dad had been out of town all week, the tank was on the red mark, and he had no idea how to put gas in his car and pay for it.

"Donnie, would you like me to go with you to the station and show you?" Mrs. West politely offered trying her best not to embarrass him any further.

"If you wouldn't mind, that would be great! I've got cash!"

This section covered some of the basic home skills young people should be exposed to before leaving the nest. I understand that you may think some of this is a bit "over the top", but I promise all the *stories are true* and checking knowledge *is important*. Sure, it may be easier and quicker to do many of these tasks yourself on a daily basis, but someone taught you ... now it's your turn to pass on the knowledge.

Leah was receiving a modest allowance for chores completed around the house. She was ten and the chores included emptying the trash cans and recycling basket, unloading the dishwasher, and daily making her bed before school. Day after day, I would enter her bedroom to find the bed unmade and the questioning would begin.

"Leah, why didn't you make your bed?"

"I don't see the point cause I'm only going to mess it up when I climb into it tonight," she calmly stated.

"But I am paying you to do that job, like my boss pays me for doing my job. If you aren't going to do it, I will have to subtract money from your allowance."

"That's cool Mom. You can keep some money because I think making my bed is dumb!"

I walked away realizing that what I thought was a great plan, had completely backfired. It's so tough being a mom.

Many teens see little value in making their bed daily so, LET IT GO! As long as they know how to make a bed, know to change sheets regularly, and that it is polite to make a bed when you are a guest at someone's house, your job is complete. His/her preference on this issue at home isn't worth the fight! Along with this idea, the matching of clothing (socks, bathing suit tops to bottoms, etc.), using a belt with pants, and tucking in a shirt (when not in a professional environment) is a thing of the past and not worth the fight.

⑦ Community

1. Where is the closest public library?

2. Who could you call in your community, if there was an emergency, other than 911?

3. Where can you find the phone numbers of the emergency agencies in your community?

4. What is a Chamber of Commerce? What is its purpose?

5. Based on where you currently live, where is the closest Chamber of Commerce office?

6. From your house, where is the closest public park and what facilities does it offer?

7. What forms of public transportation are available in your community and where can each potentially take you?

8. Take at least one form of public transportation (bus, train, subway, ferry, etc.) in your area to a predetermined destination. Have your teen research the schedule, price, pick-up/drop-off spots, etc., and then take a trip together. (I'd have lunch, go shopping or even see an exhibit. Make it fun! Remind him/her that public transportation may not run exactly on time. Also, know there are many schedules provided online and he/she may be able to download apps to help.)

⑨ Community

Funny how we can live in a community for years and rarely take advantage of all it has to offer. (I am guilty of this myself.) Bands in the park, the public library, and fall festivals at a nearby church or school, to name a few. It's like the guy who lives near the ocean and never goes in swimming or for a walk along the beach.

TC It is important to introduce and discuss local resources, activities, and opportunities that are "right in our backyards" and make sure teenagers know how to access and use neighboring resources, such as, the public library, government services, and even the Chamber of Commerce. This drives the popular point of "think global … act local".

I ask you, when was the last time you took public transportation to go somewhere? Have you needed or taken advantage of any of the services in your area that taxes help to provide? Have you ever been to a Chamber of Commerce meeting, utilized the wealth of information provided in your community newspaper (often free to residents in print or online), or used a community government website to plan an outing? What about enjoying a park or recreation center nearby?

The consequence of not knowing and not using what is available in our own community results in wasted money and time (both very valuable, if you ask me). Why spend additional money and take unnecessary time to go to a neighboring town for things that are close at hand? And since you are already paying taxes that support many government agencies in the county, why not use those resources? The internet makes this "resource" finding mission extremely easy today, so let's enlighten our teens as to *what all is out there*. These sources may also be needed in an emergency situation and we don't want to be scrambling at the crucial moment. It's nice to know where to turn, in advance.

Here's What Your Teen Needs To Know...

I. Where is the closest local library?

⑨ Answers will vary...you'll have to check this one yourself. Again, the internet, telephone books, Chamber of Commerce, and local school personnel could be helpful

I gave an assignment to my Fashion Marketing students to prepare a short report on their favorite designer. I reviewed the require-ments, told them they could use the internet, and then I shared a book from the library that had designer profiles in a two-page synopsis (even alphabetized by last name for easy access). I put the book on the desk and sent the students to work.

The students immediately headed to a computer. The book sat lonely as students searched multiple sources for the required information. Finally, Brandi walked up to my desk and asked for help as she was struggling to find what she needed. I asked if she had tried the library book. She crinkled up her forehead, rolled her eyes, picked up the book, and shuffled back to her seat. It was about ten minutes later when I noted the smile on her face as she was writing frantically.

You see, information is available on the internet, but not all data is found most easily there. Local public libraries provide a wealth of information and a larger perspective on subjects today, yet they are being used less and less each day. Make sure your teen understands that libraries have hardback books for research and pleasure reading, electronic resources (e-books, internet, etc.), and librarians/media specialists for assistance. Libraries have study rooms (for independent work or group work), magazines, newspapers, and even play areas for small children in some buildings. The stereotype of a quiet place, with no food or drink, and a librarian with a bun in her hair is a thing of the past.

Encourage an online search, with library usage, to teach young people to search more effectively. Remember that libraries are often called "Media Centers" because they have visual and media assistance and most libraries will allow a teen to get their own library card with a parent or adult at their side.

2. Who could you call in your community, if there was an emergency, other than 911?

>   Depending on the local community resources and nature of the emergency, correct answers would include as many of these as possible:
>   - Police or Sheriff Department
>   - Fire Department
>   - Poison Control
>   - Hospital ER (Emergency Room)
>   - Animal Control (if someone sees a coyote or bear in the yard, for example)
>   - FEMA (Federal Emergency Management Agency-responsible for helping citizens and first responders by planning, preparing, responding, and recovering when a disaster occurs-FEMA can be called when a flood or earthquake occurs, for example)
>   - Health Department (for questions regarding non-emergency health issues)

- Public Works (governmental group that oversees the infrastructure of a community including recreation, schools, hospitals, roads, ports, parks, beaches, water, sewage, etc.)
- Suicide Prevention Hotlines
- Water Authority
- Department of Family & Children's Services (DFACS is for reporting true abuse/neglect...not a place to vent when a teen gets mad because he/she gets grounded)

N *Make sure your teenager knows that calling 911 in the U.S. requires no area code or other digits. He/she simply needs to pick-up any telephone and when they hear the dial tone, push the numbers 9-1-1 and an operator will answer. In addition, the FCC requires all cell phone networks in the U.S. to route 911 calls to the emergency center even if the service contract has lapsed or the phone never had service. (Great use of an old phone ... just must be charged to use.) Don't fear if a phone is locked. No pin is required to dial 911 - just do it!*

Also, every country has an Emergency 911 resource number, but different digits are used for international countries. Although there are exceptions, 112, 999, and 911 are the emergency codes that most GSM/3G mobile phones have pre-programmed and are always available. Memorizing these three emergency numbers will suffice in most travel plans:

911 - North America   112 - European Union   999 - United Kingdom

Asia and Africa have several emergency numbers as do the more remote areas of the world, so check before leaving home.

3. Where can you find the phone numbers of the emergency agencies in your community?

 Telephone numbers are obtained through the yellow pages online or in a printed telephone book (often denoted on blue pages)

For online access, type in the city (or area) and the specific name of the department you are seeking. Or type "county government" or "government offices" and a very long listing of resources will appear. A hard copy phone book can also be used (if anyone still keeps those) by looking under "Government Offices" — signified by the blue page coloring.

The telephone rang in my office during my planning period and so I answered it. It is my son's 5th grade teacher (not a good sign).

"Hey Beth. Sorry to bother you. Are you in class?"

"No Jill. Is everything alright?"

"Yes. But school policy requires that I call a parent when a student ingests something strange during the day and Ben just ate some hand sanitizer."

"You've got to be kidding me. Why did he do that?" I exclaimed.

"Well, he said he was looking at it in his hand and wanted to know what it tasted like, so he tried it."

We both giggled as this was the second year she had taught Ben and she knew how his curious mind worked. Jill proceeded to tell me that he felt good, it was only a small amount, and that the nurse had been consulted … he would be fine. After we hung up the phone, I looked up the local poison control center and called myself to check on the possible side effects from eating hand sanitizer. Relieved at what I was told, I went back to work with peace of mind.

4. What is a Chamber of Commerce? What is its purpose?

A Chamber of Commerce serves as a liaison between industry and government -it serves as a community member resource on schools, businesses, and community events/activities

The goal of a Chamber is to develop, attract, expand, and retain business interests and promote a community. It serves as a networking source for new businesses and for families considering a move into the area. The Chamber houses demographics, school ratings, business statistics, and more.

5. Based on where you currently live, where is the closest Chamber of Commerce office?

Your Chamber is probably located in the 'downtown' area of the closest city-you'll have to look it up via the internet or phone book (within the government listings) if you don't already know

N Many people would say that the Chamber of Commerce isn't a viable resource today because of all the other options. Regardless, young adults need to know that the "Chamber of Commerce" exists in most towns and is utilized by local companies' marketing departments (especially small enterprises) and is open to the individual citizen to use.

It was July 2nd and had been raining for days. The kids and I were at the lake for the holiday weekend and were looking forward to taking the boat out and watching the firework display from the water. The forecast was for flooding and more rain through the 5th of July, so we devised a back-up plan with friends. If it was raining on the 4th, we would watch from their cabin-covered deck. Not a perfect view, but it could work in a pinch. Then it dawned on me, what if the weather prevented the fireworks from happening all together?

We called a few neighbors and looked online, but no status on fireworks was available. I was frustrated with the weather and the lack of information. Then, I decided to call the local Chamber of Commerce. A delightful lady informed me that the city had decided to postpone the display until the Labor Day weekend, as the forecast just offered no hope! It was that simple to get valuable information about a local event.

6. **From your house, where is the closest public park and what facilities does it offer?**

Answers will vary

Hopefully your busy life allows you some time to enjoy and get exercise in one of the community parks close to home. The local Parks and Recreation Department is in charge of maintaining these free areas that anyone can use. Facilities may include ball fields, skating areas, tennis courts, hiking and jogging trails, swimming pools, basketball courts, soccer fields, playgrounds, restrooms, picnic tables, pavilions, and even romantic interlude spots (remember those??). And lots of activities, camps, and classes for all ages!

7. What forms of public transportation are available in your community and where can each potentially take you?

⑨ Answers to this question are best discussed as options and destinations will vary depending on where one lives-hopefully, you have some form of public transportation that might include: bus, taxi, subway/tube, train, trolley, ferry, airplane, etc.-if not, discuss what transportation nearby towns and cities offer

 If a "taxi" is given as an answer to question number 7, remind your teen they are operated by private companies, but still a good transportation mode. Many areas are now offering other forms of transportation services (Uber, Lyft, SideCar, etc.). These serve as a "rideshare" or "taxi" service using an app to connect you to a local driver. You can request, ride, and pay via a mobile phone. It is extremely quick, streamlined, and provides reasonable fares. It is found around the world, in over 200+ cities.

Abby got this great fashion internship in the heart of downtown Atlanta. She was driving 50+ minutes a day from her home in the suburbs, to the heart of the city, and loving every minute of it. One Tuesday morning, her car was in the repair shop and so her mom volunteered to be her chauffeur. Shortly after Abby showed up for work, her boss told her to get across town immediately to take part in a fashion show as the designer's assistant. Her heart started to race with excitement that she had been chosen for this wonderful experience until she blurted out, "I don't have a car!"

The boss handed her the address, told her to take the bus, and walked away. Abby was paralyzed. She had never taken a metro bus and therefore ended up missing the opportunity as the boss sent someone who could complete the task. That evening, Abby's dad reminded her that managers don't have time and aren't usually willing to teach such things!

 8. Take at least one form of public transportation (bus, train, subway, ferry, etc.) in your area to a predetermined destination. Have your teen research the schedule, price, pick-up/drop-off spots, etc., and then take a trip together. (I'd have lunch, go shopping or even see an exhibit. Make it fun! Remind him/her that public transportation may not run exactly on time. Also, know there are many schedules provided online and he/she may be able to download apps to help.)

In this exercise, avoid allowing your teen to use a taxi. There is not much challenge in making a phone call, reciting an address, and sitting in the back seat while someone drives you somewhere (that is too much like what he/she did as a youngster in the back of a parent's car). Of course, if your teen avoids talking to strangers on the telephone and would struggle just to place that call or ride alone in a taxi...then there would be real value in a cab transportation exercise. I would suggest at that point to enrich the taxi trip and use a GPS to check the driver's route and honesty.

Stress the importance of getting a price ahead of time or getting an approximate idea of the average cost from point A to point B before using any form of transportation. And don't forget to take time to discuss safety precautions when using public transportation.

Traveling as a family is always an adventure. Our trip west for a niece's wedding proved to be a good example of this, right from the get go. Our plans included flying into Las Vegas and staying for two days before heading to the national park areas. When I made our Vegas hotel reservation, I had inquired about the cost of a taxi ride from the airport to the hotel and was told it would be $18 — $20. We mapped out our next 10 days in the parks and anxiously waited for the departure date.

Many taxi departure sites have set fee structures that are posted to provide guidance to travelers. The posted fee may be to a given area, hotel, or tourist spot. Look for them.

We landed in Las Vegas on time, gathered our luggage at the airport, and hailed a taxi at the taxi stand. About 20 minutes into the ride, my husband and I exchanged glances as the taxi meter was reading $20.40, $22.00, $24.80, $27.10, $29.30. My children had never ridden in a taxi and so they found this whole adventure rather fascinating until we heard a police siren behind us. My daughter turned pale and grabbed my hand.

The cab driver pulled over and put down his window as the officer approached. The officer leaned in the window and asked us where we were headed. My husband gave the name of our hotel and asked the officer if there was a problem. The officer said, "Yes, sir! This driver is taking you on a joy ride to increase the fare. My department has been running a sting to catch and stop innocent people like you from being taken advantage of when visiting our town. I will be following you to the hotel and will deal with this man at that time as to not delay your arrival any further. And there will be no charge for this service."

We exchanged glances again and cracked a small smile. We thought something was fishy when the meter got to the $29.00 mark. Needless to say, no tip was given for this ride and checking ahead on costs (with some help from the local law enforcement) really did pay off!

My advice in preparing teens for adulthood would include teaching him/her to use multiple forms of transportation and community resources. Explore the public library with young children, so as teens they already feel comfortable there. Talk about the multitude of government agencies available to the masses in your community. Visit the Chamber. See if your Parks and Recreation Department has a disc golf course, skate board park, dog park, walking trail or a fitness circuit to try. Be on alert for free concerts or when the carnival/fair comes to town.

Let your teen lead an excursion the next time you go out with them. Consider using a transportation mode other than your car and act like a shadow while he/she leads (in case he/she gets really off the beaten path). It may take more effort, but the pay-off is of huge benefit.

Remember to teach that some public transportation accepts only cash (and exact change at that), so carrying a debit card only (teens love that debit card) isn't enough! Bills and coins should be in his/her pocket or purse at all times.

The younger generation is not going to embrace going to the library in the same way as you and past generations did, so LET IT GO! You can be a role model and suggest using it, but understand that teens today truly believe that everything they need is found through their electronic devices (a point that is hard to argue for long). Teenagers will most likely only use a library's resources through online access and download offerings.

⑦ General Government

1. How old must you be to vote?

2. What are the requirements to be able to register to vote?

3. When you register to vote, you will be asked to affiliate yourself with a "party" (Note: not always required except to vote in certain types of elections). What are the names of these party options?

4. In your community, where exactly would you go to vote in an election?

 5. Why is it important to vote?

6. Name the current President and Vice President of the United States.

7. What are the three branches of the U.S. Government?

8. What is meant by "Checks and Balances" in government?

9. In your state, how many U.S. Senators are there?

10. In your state, how many members are there in the U.S. House of Representatives?

11. The Senate and House of Representatives makeup what governmental body?

⑨ General Government

Have you ever seen the *Jimmy Kimmel Show,* a YouTube clip, or the TV show *20/20,* when random people are stopped on the street and asked questions about their government? Writers have no trouble creating monologue jokes or ten minute story segments after showing a scene where the average resident, of various ages, is stumped by questions about the government. Questions as basic as who is the Vice President of the United States? Who makes up Congress? How many senators exist in your home state? Some people have even lost out on winning money as part of a game challenge because of their inability to call to mind names and facts such as these. (Gotta hate that!)

What's ironic is that we all learned this government information at some point in school. Yet, individuals tend to not be able to recall it when asked, and it is awkward. In addition, many teens don't read newspapers or watch television news to keep abreast of these current event issues. This results in teens have nothing to contribute when political topics surface during conversations with adults. (Rather sad, I'd say.)

I know politics is supposed to be a topic to avoid in public and private settings, but I'm not talking about debating political issues. I am suggesting that teenagers need to know the basics of how the government is set-up, who is currently in charge, and what the government can do for them. That's why you are asking your teen about these things in this section.

Make sure teens can pull basic governmental particulars to the forefront of his/her brain and stay current of general facts. Teenagers need to know voting procedures and that this privilege, matters (and not just on the presidential level). I have come to realize that many teens don't understand that congressmen vote on issues that impact *their* lives. Let's start exposing teens to the elected officials he/she can go to for assistance and support of their beliefs. If not educated in these matters, teens become adults that don't participate in the constitutional rights and responsibilities of a democratic society.

Here's What Your Teen Needs To Know...

1. How old must you be to vote?

   18 years old

2. What are the requirements to be able to register to vote?

   One must be a citizen of the U.S., a resident of the state in which he/she will be voting, and have a valid photo ID with his/her name and address on it (check state guidelines for what is an accepted ID where you reside)

Voting is a right that many young people don't exercise in this country today. High schools have started to promote voter registration opportunities during the school day to encourage teens to vote. Anyone who interacts with teens should also be encouraging teens to take the steps to engage in this American right, especially with the ease of online registration. Although the laws vary some from state to state, typically an 18 year old can register as late as 30 days prior to an election. (You may need to research the requirements for where you live.) What an individual needs is a picture identification which can be in the form of a photo license, passport, student or employee ID. Additionally, proof of residency is typically required and can be a bill, bank statement, paycheck, or the like, as long as the name matches the ID and has an address on it. Again, this may vary by state, so check the specifics in your area. Sources for more information and to register are easily obtained on the internet or through government offices.

3. When you register to vote, you will be asked to affiliate yourself with a "party" (Note: not always required except to vote in certain types of elections). What are the names of these party options?

⑨ Republican and Democratic are the two major parties-the "third" parties include, but are not limited to, Constitution, Green, and Libertarian

I am not here to touch on the pros and cons of political parties. Nor am I willing to get into politics within your inner circle. However, I would like adults to help teens research and make an informed decision on his/her political views and party affiliation. The important thing is that he/she realizes they have been given a gift of living in a country that allows opinions to count and everyone should participate.

4. In your community, where exactly would you go to vote in an election?

 Answers vary-It may be a local school, church or community building

Individuals will be assigned a voting poll site after registering to vote. The polling precinct may be found on a voter registration card, sent in the mail, or researched online ... so no worries.

5. Why is it important to vote?

 Answers vary

This discussion question can trail off in many directions, hence the need to discuss. I would expect that comments might include the belief that through voting, citizens help influence change. These changes relate to health, wealth, social issues, and civil rights.

Another response may revolve around the idea that voting is a right given to citizens through the U.S. Constitution as part of a democracy. Since it hasn't always been a right for everyone, that makes it more sacred and compelling.

Or teens may see voting as a "pledge of support" (or lack of support) to the actions taken by elected government officials. Thereby, assisting the government to know how to function according to voter's wishes and needs. Because of limited experience with government, teens today will need you to point out that there is always a chance that he/she may someday need the official they helped vote into office (i.e., you need to appear in front of a newly elected judge or congressperson in your area to help expedite a passport, get a White House tour, or request a new stop sign in your neighborhood).

Please include in this conversation that voting is not a game. It is a private issue and teens don't have to vote for the same individuals as their friends or family. Stress the importance of doing research on candidates and not buying strictly into the information provided in TV ads. It is also important for one to not vote solely on a single issue (a tendency of young people). Practicality tells us that we can't have everything we want in the platform of a single candidate, so stress weighing all of a candidate's positions on a variety of issues before placing a vote.

Lastly, maybe your teen would like and benefit from volunteering at the local polling site to learn more. And remind him/her that when they go to college or join the military, they can still vote using the absentee ballot system, so no excuses!

6. Name the current President and Vice President of the United States.

   (?) Research for current names of these leaders

7. What are the three branches of the U.S. Government?

   (?) Legislative, Executive, Judicial

The Cabinet consists of the heads of the 15 major departments of the government. The Supreme Court is made up of nine justices, eight which are associate justices and one is named as the chief justice (nominated by the President and approved by the Senate).

In case you want to dive in further, here is a brief synopsis of what each branch does:

- The Legislative branch (consisting of the House of Representatives and the Senate) must write, discuss, and make laws.
- The Executive branch (consisting of the President, Vice President, and Cabinet) must implement and enforce laws.
- The Judicial branch (consisting of the Supreme Court and other federal courts) evaluate and interpret laws to ensure they are constitutional.

8. What is meant by "Checks and Balances" in government?

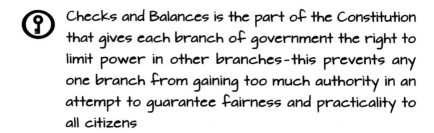

Checks and Balances is the part of the Constitution that gives each branch of government the right to limit power in other branches - this prevents any one branch from gaining too much authority in an attempt to guarantee fairness and practicality to all citizens

Knowing the short answer here isn't enough for understanding, so make sure you dig for true comprehension. Teens should know that rarely does the government need to implement the Checks and Balance policy. However, here are a few *examples* of how the United States government could implement this necessary practice:

1. The President (Executive Branch) vetos a law that was passed by Congress which then stops the law from being enacted.
2. Congress overrides a presidential veto by having a 2/3 majority vote in both houses.
3. Congress and the President can take action to lessen, or even negate, a Supreme Court ruling by passing a new law or amending an old law to improve it.
4. Congress must declare war according to the constitution, even though the President is the Commander in Chief of the armed forces.
5. The President appoints his/her cabinet members, but the Senate approves the choice(s).

9. In your state, how many U.S. Senators are there?

 2...for a total of 100 in the United States

These government officials are elected and may remain in office for six years. (Can anyone name one of their state's U.S. senators for extra credit???)

10. In your state, how many members are there in the U.S. House of Representatives?

 Varies by state

This was sort of a trick question. There are currently 435 in total (as of 2010 census), but the number of representatives per state can change. The allowed number of representatives is based on the census population data and the number of districts each state is then awarded. So, the total number per state may change every ten years.

The minimum is one (regardless of population) and the members of the House are elected for a two-year term. Look online to find the current number in your state, to be sure.

11. **The Senate and House of Representatives makeup what government body?**

 **The Congress**

It is doubtful that your teen will ever get stopped on the street by a TV host and asked questions related to his/her government, but that doesn't mean a little review of current events and discussions of governmental protocol isn't in order from time to time. Think of it as a history review or just relish hearing the thoughts and ideas that fill your teen's head related to government today. Don't make this about political issues. Keep an open mind and heart to help build a foundation of knowledge that he/she can build upon.

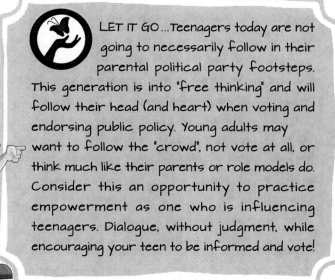

LET IT GO...Teenagers today are not going to necessarily follow in their parental political party footsteps. This generation is into "free thinking" and will follow their head (and heart) when voting and endorsing public policy. Young adults may want to follow the "crowd", not vote at all, or think much like their parents or role models do. Consider this an opportunity to practice empowerment as one who is influencing teenagers. Dialogue, without judgment, while encouraging your teen to be informed and vote!

⑦ Study Habits

1. Define study skills.

2. Do you believe that you know how to study and practice good study habits/skills?

3. Name a minimum of five things to consider about your *environment* when practicing good study habit skills.

4. Name a minimum of five *techniques* to consider when practicing good study habit skills.

5. Describe your environment when you study.

6. What time of the day do you do most of your studying?

7. How long do you typically study each night?

8. Do you believe your current grades are a good reflection of your effort?

 9. Demonstrate how to outline the following few paragraphs. Use proper outline form that includes indents, numbering, and lettering.

Study Habits

Study habits start with good study skills. Study skills are the techniques implemented when learning something new, retaining information, and preparing for assessments (tests or evaluations). Good study habits help learners through an organized approach that will lead to success in school as well as any time one is trying to master something new in life. Study skills aid a learner by allowing them to build on previous knowledge and apply concepts to new or similar situations, basically taking short-term information and turning it into long-term understanding. Although study skills may not come naturally, these skills can be learned. Benefits of developing these skills include saving time, building confidence, reducing stress, increasing creativity, and school/career success.

It has been said that we remember 10% of what we read, 20% of what we hear, and 30% of what we see. When we combine what we see and hear, 50% is retained, which is a significant increase. This is due to the fact that 11% of learning takes place through what is heard and 83% through what is seen.[3] Which is why sleeping through your teacher's power point presentation while he/she is lecturing is a bad idea. Instead, try reading class notes out loud in your room. Seeing the notes and hearing them at the same time will increase retention just like orally quizzing a friend using a practice test or notes is a viable alternative to silent study. And if a learner talks about a task as they are doing it (basically demonstrating while verbally reviewing what is occurring), as much as 90% will be committed to memory because the senses of seeing, hearing, talking, and doing are all being utilized.

---

3 Jain, Vishal. (September 10, 2008) "Study Skills for School Success." Retrieved on: Date from Full Web Address, starting with http://schoolofeducators.com/tag/study-skills-definition/

Concentrating on one fact for a long time or writing it over and over will help convert it to the goal of long-term memory. This is why when you first meet someone and want to learn their name, you should repeat it, use the name several times, and/or associate the name with something familiar. Guaranteed to improve the likelihood of you recalling that name the next time you meet.

Additionally, a person with good study skills will have all the needed supplies ready and available when he/she sits down to study (computer, pens, pencils, calculator, notebook, book, etc.). Popping up continuously to get supplies will waste time and energy and break concentration. Learners who use colored folders and/or notebooks with tabs to keep paperwork organized will find easier access when studying… and don't forget to add titles and dates to all notes.

Your study area should be free of distractions (e.g., TV, cell phone, radio, non-studying individuals, and computer use not related to task). It should be spacious, with good lighting, and ventilation. Make the area comfortable, but not so comfortable that you take a nap instead!

Anyone can become a person with good study habits with just a little effort. Start today!

⑨ Study Habits

When I taught, I found teens frequently misspelled the word "interest". They always seemed to forget that first "e" and would write "intrest" (like it sounded to them). Since spelling was not my strong suit, I would joke with my students and tell them that "if I caught an error in spelling, you must have really messed up!" It was through humor that I was able to reach adolescents and increase their learning. It was also through teaching good study skill habits and demanding students practice these skills (e.g., requiring a graded notebook with dividers, labels, dates, and in chronological order) that all students improved their performance. Now it's your turn to check the study skill habits of your teen.

TC Most of us are not born with the inclination for organization and good study habits. However, learning for the long-term relies upon building on past skills while turning short-range knowledge into foundational blocks (i.e., one could not master chemistry or physics without first learning and recalling certain math skills). *The good news is that study skills can be learned!* Therefore, adolescents have no excuse for not using these strategies. Putting in some extra effort when learning will improve one's success throughout life.

Too often, study skills aren't taught at home or early enough in one's educational career. Yet, teachers, professors in college, and even bosses will expect their people to have these skills. After all, learning company procedures, doing taxes, filling out a loan application, and comprehending a house contract for the first time, demands a person to recall information (specific information, at that). Recall is a form of study, in or out of a school building.

Some teachers, as early as kindergarten, will lead by example and implement study skill practices as part of their expectations and class set-up. Examples of this would be using color-coded folders for the different subject areas (social studies is blue, reading is red, science is yellow, etc.), using flash cards (for spelling words), or outlining notes on the board. (Do you remember anything like that from your child's elementary school days or even your own?) Fortunately, many kids pick up on these practices and continue the pattern as they get older (typically the higher functioning students). Regrettably, study skill techniques are not part of any required curriculum, as such. Extra attention and study tips may be given to students in school, but many learners often fall through the cracks when it comes to mastering these skills. That is why you, as the adult influence, need to ensure these skills are shared and encouraged. If you don't feel qualified to help your teen with these skills, there are many outside resources on the internet, at your teen's school, at the local library, and through private tutors. And although this book is targeted to those adults working with teens, I suggest you share this wisdom with those adults who have younger children (or the younger children themselves) because the earlier he/she starts, the better.

Here's What Your Teen Needs To Know...

1. Define study skills.

(?) Answers may vary but should be something like these: approaches used to learn, methods and techniques that help in school, strategies to learn, steps taken to learn through an organized approach, tips for test taking

The exactness of the definition isn't what is important. Your teen acknowledging that study skills are the things done to aid and improve their capacity for learning is what you want to take from their response. Typically, students will tie the definition to school learning even though study skills can be used anywhere retention and learning is expected or evaluated.

If your teen adds that study skills allow use of their time and resources most efficiently, that would be a bonus answer and an indication of real understanding and perhaps even the use of true study skills in their lives.

2. Do you believe that you know and practice good study habits/skills?

> Answers will vary to include: yes, no, sometimes...and there can be two different replies for 'knowing' and 'practicing' (a key distinction)

This is a good starter question to get your teen to reflect on his/her personal study skills. Some young people will admit to knowing the skills to use, but not practicing them. Sadder yet is the acknowledgement of *not knowing how* to best study and learn something efficiently. Think of the struggle and frustration that the "not knowing" child could have avoided through the years had they been able to develop good habits from the get-go.

3. Name a minimum of five things to consider about your *environment* when practicing good study habit skills.

⑨ Here is a list of several ideas, but give credit for any reasonable idea given:
- good lighting
- spacious and void of clutter
- comfortable sitting area (not too comfortable like a bed...too tempting to nap)
- area to walk or move around in, if needed
- use of a table or desk
- limited distractions (electronics, non-studying people, etc.)
- supplies at hand (writing utensils, books, computer, highlighters, calculator, etc.)
- use of a cell phone only as an study aid (e.g., recording, internet, and dictionary app)...avoiding email, social media and phone calls unless on a break
- good ventilation
- sitting near the front in a classroom or lecture hall to help focus and attention

Natural lighting is best. However, if that isn't feasible, use an ordinary lamp, overhead light or desk light. The important thing is that the light is bright with focus on the work area. If you are right-handed, place the lamp to the left side to avoid shadows. Consider using fluorescent bulbs over incandescent bulbs because they last longer, save electricity, and are available in various colors (light colors are best for your eyes). Halogen bulbs are considered best for illuminating reading material. Since the choice isn't always ours to make, do your best for the situation.

4. Name a minimum of five *techniques* to consider when practicing good study habit skills.

Here is a list of several ideas, but give credit for any reasonable idea given:
- plan and organize materials for ease in accessing data
- use a calendar or agenda for scheduling and prioritizing
- use notebooks or folders with dividers or sections
- use loose-leaf paper for flexibility (avoid spiral notebooks)
- use wide margins on notes (for additional notations)
- label & date handouts and notes
- write clear, concise notes (outline format) to discriminate types of information
- use standard abbreviations in notes (allows you to write faster as long as you know what they mean)
- color code information in notebooks, on flash cards, and on notes
- use highlighters of different colors
- keep a list of questions and get answers by utilizing teachers, professors, friends, books, notes, internet, etc.
- use graphic organizers to create spatial connections & build on ideas (also called mapping)
- use note cards or flash cards
- recall and review over several days, not just one time or one night
- visualize

- relate information to previous learning
- use repetition
- mix the use of auditory (oral & listening), visual (seeing), and kinesthetic (doing)
- know your best style of learning
- use acronyms or mnemonics to recall (ex: FIFO- first in, first out OR Every Good Boy Does Fine -notes on a music scale: E G B D F)

The best study strategies to use often depend on whether you are seeking to put information into long or short-term memory. I encourage you to do more research on this subject.

- know the exam format (multiple choice, short answer, fill-in-the-blanks, etc.)
- summarize (2-3 sentences) what you learned (orally or in written format)
- quiz yourself and others
- utilize the skim, question, re-read, recall, and review reading method
- study in the same, regular place
- take periodic breaks (suggestion: 30 minutes of studying, 3 minute break, 2 minutes of review and then plan what is coming next)
- hydrate with water (your brain gets thirsty...avoid caffeine as the only liquid)

5. Describe your environment when you study.

 Answers will vary.

Make sure comments are made that include lighting, noise level, distractions present, furniture he/she likes to sit or lay upon, presence of others, if there is a desk or table involved, tools/supplies at hand, etc. Avoid judgment.

6. What time of the day do you do most of your studying?

 Answers will vary

Wish I could state the "perfect" time to study, but I can't. The truth is, studying is completely an individual choice. Personality, resources, time, sleep cycles, and other demands (jobs, school, family, friends, etc.) can dictate the time of day a person can and should study, so let your teen determine his/her own studying time schedule as long as the results are positive.

Encourage teens (in fact, encourage any learner, no matter the age) to experiment with the time of day he/she studies and see when

As a teacher, I would remind students that typically a person's capacity to make decisions deteriorates over the course of a day. (Evident in most 7th period classes and decisions made by adults late at night! - LOL) Therefore, I encouraged my students to try and do more cognitive or practice-based studying earlier in the day to enhance the outcome. Rote memorization doesn't involve decisions, so that can be better suited for the evening.

they are most productive. Some students need to do their homeowork and study right after school while they are still in the school mode. Others need a break first. Some are morning people and will be half asleep by 8:00 pm if they try to study then. Others experience the opposite effect. Time of day can also correlate with the subject matter. Here is a perfect story illustrating what I learned about my own daughter's study habits ...

 My son, Ben, was sitting beside Leah, on the sofa in the family room. He was being the good big brother and had been tutoring her in calculus for over a month. Suddenly, Leah bursts into tears. Ben quickly stated, "There is no crying in Calculus, Leah! The answer is on the page in front of you. Think about it!"
"Ben, I just can't do math after 9 o'clock at night!!"

7. **How long do you typically study each night?**

 Answers vary

The response here could range from ten minutes to five hours or more. Again, there is no perfect answer. Depending on the ability level of an individual, the subject matter, desired results, what task/information is being mastered, previous experience or knowledge of the subject, requirements from whomever/whatever is doing the teaching, time available, age or grade level ... time required will be different. (Boy, that is a lot of factors!) Furthermore, study time can

N *I was always told in college that the rule of thumb for success was "for every hour of class time, one should be spending five hours out of class on that subject". (Can't say I always did that, but at least I was aware of the commitment possibly needed.)*

change from night to night. (However, if a high school student tells you he/she is averaging 20 minutes a night... they definitely could and should do more! That's just a fact about high school demands.)

I also can tell you that numerous students confided in me, on many occasions, that he/she reaped the benefits of studying multiple days/times in short bursts... a more effective approach than a long cram session and certainly more effective than an "all-nighter". (That has always been what I was taught in my education courses and what I experienced personally too. How about you?) It's like eating several small meals to maintain continuous energy instead of a large meal, one time.

8. Do you believe your current grades are a good reflection of your effort?

> Answers vary-hopefully, you can tell when your teen stretches the truth because teens tend to fib a little on this answer

 9. Demonstrate how to outline the following few paragraphs. Use proper outline form that includes indents, numbering, and lettering.

<u>Study Habits</u>

Study habits start with good study skills. Study skills are the techniques implemented when learning something new, retaining information, and preparing for assessments (tests or evaluations). Good study habits help learners through an organized approach that will lead to success in school as well as any time one is trying to master something new in life. Study skills aid a learner by allowing them to build on previous knowledge and apply concepts to new or similar situations, basically taking short-term information and turning it into long-term understanding. Although study skills may not come naturally, these skills can be learned. Benefits of developing these skills include saving time, building confidence, reducing stress, increasing creativity, and school/career success.

It has been said that we remember 10% of what we read, 20% of what we hear, and 30% of what we see. When we combine what we see and hear, 50% is retained, which is a significant increase. This is due to the fact that 11% of learning takes place through what is heard and 83% through what is seen. Which is why sleeping through your teacher's power point presentation while he/she is lecturing is a bad idea. Instead, try reading class notes out loud in your room. Seeing the notes and hearing them at the same time will increase retention just like orally quizzing a friend using a practice test or notes is a viable alternative to silent study. And if a learner talks about a task as they are doing it (basically demonstrating while verbally reviewing what is occurring), as much as 90% will be committed to memory because the senses of seeing, hearing, talking, and doing are all being utilized.

Concentrating on one fact for a long time or writing it over and over will help convert it to the goal of long-term memory. This is why when you first meet someone and want to learn their name, you should repeat it, use the name several times, and/or associate the name with something familiar. Guaranteed to improve the likelihood of you recalling that name the next time you meet.

Additionally, a person with good study skills will have all the needed supplies ready and available when he/she sits down to study (computer, pens, pencils, calculator, notebook, book, etc.). Popping up continuously to get supplies will waste time and energy and break concentration. Learners who use colored folders and/or notebooks with tabs to keep paperwork organized will find easier access when studying... and don't forget to add titles and dates to all notes.

Your study area should be free of distractions (e.g., TV, cell phone, radio, non-studying individuals and computer use not related to task). It should be spacious, with good lighting, and ventilation. Make the area comfortable, but not so comfortable that you take a nap instead!

Anyone can become a person with good study habits with just a little effort. Start today!

 Here is generally what the outline should look like:

Study Habits

I. Study Skills
   A. Definition: steps taken to improve a learner's capacity to learn through an organized approach
   B. Study skills help you:
      1. learn something new
      2. retain information
      3. turn short-term data into long-term understanding
      4. handle assessments
      5. build on previous knowledge
      6. apply concepts to new or similar situations
   C. Can be learned
   D. Benefits include:
      1. saves time
      2. builds confidence
      3. reduces stress
      4. increases creativity

    5. school success

    6. career success

II. Statistics of the experts

    A. we remember 10% of what we read

    B. we remember 20% of what we hear

    C. we remember 30% of what we see

    D. combining improves learning even more

       I. 50% is retained if we see and hear information

         a.) 11% of learning takes place through hearing

         b.) 83% of learning comes through sight

       2. as much as 90% will be committed to our memories if we see, hear, talk, and do all at the same time

III. Good study skill pointers

    A. concentrate for a long time on I fact

    B. rewrite facts repeatedly

    C. have supplies ready

    D. use colored folders and notebooks (with tabs)

    E. label and date everything for organization

    F. study area should be:

       I. free of distractions

         a.) cell phones

         b.) tv/music

         c.) non-studiers

         d.) non-related computer use

Outlining "rules" state that if there is a "I" in the outline, there must be a "II". If there is an "A", there must be a "B" and so forth. This is important if an outline is to be turned in for a grade. Otherwise, indents with lettering and numbering sequentially will help any note taking endeavor and provide a great tool for studying.

2. spacious
3. have good lighting
4. have good ventilation
5. be comfortable

I was always amazed at how many students would struggle when the class assignment involved outlining a chapter from their book. I would walk around the room, glancing at everything from paragraphs to papers that had only lists of the bolded headings copied from the book. Often I would stop class and review how to outline on the whiteboard. Some students told me that they were never taught to outline formally. Taking that knowledge into account, know that this outline is only a guide for you to compare to your teen's outline and look for positive signs of proper outlining to praise. He/she may not have the exact format as illustrated in the sample, but hopefully you will see the use of indentations, lettering, and numbering, and that's a start.

Point out to your teenager that *not every word from the paragraph is put in the outline (e.g.,* the nap joke in the passage). Authors tend to use humor to make a point memorable. It is not necessary information to include on an outline, as it isn't something that will be found on a future quiz/test or in life use. Teens typically think they *must* include every word in some way (similar to highlighting every sentence in a passage). Learners will need to practice evaluating key points within a reading section and time will make them a more skilled assessor of information.

You should look for an outline that includes indents for each subheading with lettering/numbering sequences that support the heading or point above it. Remind your teen that paraphrasing can be used as long as the facts are stated. Another option for the outline is to add color coding with highlighters (especially for visual learners). For example, all roman number points are in yellow. All capital A, B, C, etc., sub-headings are blue, and so on. Many students use just one or two colors to emphasize key topics. Coloring all the words on a page has little value. (It's like teens sometimes highlight so much because they miss the coloring worksheets that stopped after second grade. — LOL)

Below is a *generic outline format*. The main ideas take roman numerals. Sub-points, under each main idea, take capital letters and are indented and support the main idea. Additional important points need to be indented further and placed under the capital letters and are preceded with numbers. And the pattern continues.

I. MAIN IDEA
   A. Supplementary point or supporting idea to I
   B. A second supplementary idea or supporting idea to I
      1. Subsidiary idea to B
      2. Subsidiary idea to B
         a.) Additional point relating to 2
         b.) Another point relating to 2
II. MAIN IDEA
   A. Supplementary point or supporting idea to II
   B. Another point or idea to II
III. MAIN IDEA
** and the outline continues

When doing an outline, concentrate on facts found in the passages that are listed in bold, italics, headings or first lines in a new paragraph.

This has been an overview of study habits/skills. I hope your take-away includes that organization of study material is crucial to saving time and feeling confident. So many smart and capable students get poor grades because they don't turn in completed assignments on the due date or at all. Teens will do the work, but then don't know where they put the papers! (Submitting online assignments is helping some of that, but students will still forget to "send".) I encourage you to guide teenagers to attempt some new study skill strategies, remembering that one strategy does not fit all learning goals. Have your teen discard strategies that don't work and find a new or replacement technique to try... keeping the ones that work and turning them into **habits!**

Today, kids aren't going to use a paper agenda or calendar to keep important dates and information organized, so LET IT GO! The electronic age has wonderful alternatives to paper. So, encourage your teen to use the "calendar" or "to do" list of their choice. They can even help you convert to using one if you haven't done so already. The key here is to use something daily to stay organized!

Wrap-Up

Well, you did it! I assume if you are reading this last section, the questions have been asked. There has been an increase in awareness of subjects requiring instruction or a refresher course needed by your teen(s). And life has just become a little easier, with less negative consequences, and more success for several adolescents. And I bet you learned a few things yourself and enjoyed talking with your teen more than you expected! How cool is that?

Now, don't let the dialogue stop. Keep asking questions and preparing your teen for the real world. **Look forward to Book 2, in the L.I.F.E. series, and** *Challenge Your Teen's Social Skills.* Book 2 will cover topics including general etiquette (introductions, handshakes, thank-you notes, etc.), dining etiquette (tipping, table settings, meal manners, etc.), written communication (letter formats, addressing envelopes, emailing guidelines, etc.) and oral communication (cell phone rules, speech, call inquiries, etc.). These topics will result in some challenging discussions. **Book 3 will** *Challenge Your Teen's Independence Readiness* by checking job seeking skills, finance/money management, college preparation and travel expectations. These can be the final check points before the teen bird flies from the nest.

You know, I've always believed teenagers don't get enough credit for being wonderful human beings. If you take the time to interact with them, they are creative, fun, unique, and so worth your time. I hope this book has generated the same experience and opinion for you.

Additional Information

www.learninginfoforeveryday.com

www.facebook.com/learninginfoforeveryday

@beth_life_

Books available online in paperback and eBook versions and at select brick and mortar bookstores.

If your group is interested in a personal appearance or speaking engagement, contact me at beth@learninginfoforeveryday.com

Acknowledgements

I would like to thank my husband, Tom, who has always been my biggest supporter, best friend, and believed that I was making a difference in the lives of many young people even when I wasn't sure.

I want to thank my children, Benjamin and Leah, who supplied not only material for this book, but who make it easy to be a mom and a teacher in their lives. Thanks for listening ... at least most of the time.

To my parents, Joe and Janet, for teaching me the importance of striving to do a quality job, not an average job, in all endeavors.

To Augustina, Jason, Mary Helen, Sue, Kerith, Nancy, Linda, Lisa, and Sam for providing honest feedback and insight into various aspects of this whole writing adventure. I learned a lot and will continue to pay attention if you are willing to share.

To all my friends, family, and colleagues who shared teen stories, observations, and concerns with me. You supplied content for this book, whether you realize it or not.

And last, but not least, I am thankful everyday to those teens who enriched my life by letting me share a part of theirs. You kept me young at heart, kept laughter in my day, and made each week a true learning experience ... for us both.

About The Author

Beth Carey is a retired teacher from the Atlanta, Georgia, area with a passion for aiding teenagers as they prepare for life. Her mission in and out of the classroom has always been to help teens with their journey into the real world so they become happy, responsible, independent adults.

She received an undergraduate degree in marketing education from Indiana University of Pennsylvania and master's degree from Georgia State University in vocational leadership. She taught high school in various states during her 30-year tenure and was awarded Georgia Marketing Teacher of the Year in 2006 and voted by her peers to receive Teacher of the Year at her home high school in 2011. Her students earned multiple awards on the regional, state, and international level of competition through their involvement in the Association of Marketing Students (DECA), under her leadership. Her ability to use a dose of daily humor and love while setting high expectations and limits in the classroom allowed teens to thrive. Her focus was giving teenagers understanding and real life problem-solving skills related to the world of business.

When not with adolescents, Beth loves to cook, travel, and spend time with her husband and children at the lake. She invites you to "Challenge" Your Teen's Basic Knowledge, Social Skills, and Independence Readiness. *L.I.F.E. (Learning Information For Everyday)* is a book series targeting other adults who share her goals.

Beth would love to hear your thoughts, stories and suggestions, so feel free to contact her at www.learninginfoforeveryday.com or beth@learninginfoforeveryday.com.

CPSIA information can be obtained at www.ICGtesting.com
Printed in the USA
LVOW10s0824260416

485236LV00002B/3/P